Oh, to Be Woman

Ode to the Wild, Sacred & Worthy Within

This book was written, envisioned, and crafted by the author, with digital tools used solely for organization, and editorial polishing.

Published by Golden Veil Press
ISBN: [978-1-9193355-7-5]

Acknowledgement

First, I thank the woman I see in the mirror—
and every version of her who walked before me
Some feel like strangers now,
yet each carried a piece of the story that brought me here
They showed up, again and again,
even when the way forward was uncertain
They walked through fire and still kept their hearts open
They dared to unbecome and become, a thousand times over

To my parents—
Thank you for loving me wholeheartedly
For trusting me enough to give me freedom,
for letting me make my own mistakes,
and for always being there to help me rise from them
Even when my path was unfamiliar to you, you stood by me
Your quiet support has been the ground beneath my feet

And to every soul who crossed my path,
whether as a guide, a mirror, or a challenge—
you have all been my teachers
This book is a reflection of the life I've lived,
and the life I've chosen to create

A Soft Beginning

Oh, how I love being a woman—
not just in the obvious ways,
but in the quiet, holy ache of it
In the way we feel deeply,
break open and bloom
In the way our bodies remember
even when our minds forget

This book is not a manual—
it is a mirror, a ceremony, a reclamation
It won't tell you who to become;
it will walk beside you
as you remember who you've always been

You may be standing at the edge of a life
you no longer fit into—
a version of yourself you've silently outgrown
Let these pages show you the way

Here, you will move through four sacred phases,
each a threshold inviting you deeper into your truth

You'll be asked to let go
To grieve
To soften
To rise
To reclaim

To live as if your life were a love letter
to the woman you were always meant to be

By the end of this journey,
you may not recognize the woman you were—
and you won't need to
Because what's waiting for you
is a life so true,
so full,
so wildly yours,
it may stretch beyond what you currently dare to dream

You don't need to know how it all unfolds—
only to say *yes*
to the first soft step

Let's begin

CONTENTS

PHASE 1: THE SACRED UNRAVELING

There is wisdom in the unraveling
In following the ache back to its origin
In listening for the echoes that shaped the woman you became

This is not undoing for the sake of collapse
It is a descent into deeper knowing
A remembering of how your patterns were born
and why they clung so tightly to you

Though these pages speak often through the language of love
it is not only love that is being undone
It is every place you once sought yourself outside yourself
in attention, in approval, in promises, in potential

Love is simply where it first hurt
But the lessons here reach far beyond—
into family, culture, ancestry,
even the stories you whisper only to yourself in silence

This unraveling is the preparation
Every thread you loosen becomes fertile ground
where truth can rise again, steady as breath,
rooted as bone, inevitable as dawn

The Illusion of Holding On

You may be someone
who believed love meant holding on—
to people, to stories,
to almosts that never became
and forevers that never stayed

You clung, not because you were weak,
but because you were taught
that letting go was abandonment
and holding on through thick and thin was devotion

So you tightened your grip
held breath where softness longed to flow
stayed longer than the truth required

But this one beautiful life does not ask for your suffering
It does not thrive in fists closed around what is already gone
It does not demand you to disappear to keep love alive

To let go is not to abandon
It is to choose peace over chaos,
truth over illusion,
and self over survival

This is the beginning of a different kind of love—
one that never costs you your wholeness

Let this be the moment
you unclench the story,
exhale the weight,
and return—open-hearted—to yourself

The Ache That Calls You Home

There is a longing we rarely name
It hums beneath our beauty, our brilliance
even our confidence

A quiet ache to be seen without performance
to be held without having to earn it
to be chosen without shrinking

For many of us, this ache shaped everything
It taught us how to mold, how to reach
how to read the room before we ever read ourselves

This was survival
We learned to dim to feel safe
to give more than we had
to explain ourselves before anyone even asked
to override our knowing just to keep the peace

And so we attached and we chased
not just the person in front of us
but the feeling they evoked
the echo of something familiar
the shape of a wound we forgot we carried

Attachment often dresses itself as love
But its roots are older, deeper
Sometimes ancestral

The memory they stir
by accident or by design—
is a doorway, a mirror

a haunting of the places where love once felt inconsistent,
withheld, or conditional

And without even realizing it
we seek resolution in the faces
that resemble the original rupture

But this is not your fault
It is your pattern
And patterns can be rewritten

Because the ache is not proof that something is broken
It is a sacred signal
not to try harder
but to come home

Longing Is Not Love

The ache calls you home—
but sometimes, instead of answering,
we mistake its hunger for love itself

We often confuse longing with love
intensity with intimacy
the emotional highs and lows
the adrenaline of almosts for passion

But that's not connection
That's a nervous system mistaking chaos for chemistry

Real love feels steady, soft
sometimes even quiet
And when you've grown used to chasing
that kind of care can feel boring—
not because it is
but because it doesn't match the frequency of your wound

Next time you yearn for someone
ask yourself gently—
is this love calling me home
or am I trying to earn it again?

Because love—
real love—
does not need convincing
It meets you
It chooses you
It stays

The Red Flags We Paint Pink

They said they weren't ready
but you heard *"not yet"*
They pulled away, and you chased harder—
hoping love would convince them
They dismissed your needs
but you called it compromise

Sometimes we do see the red flags
We just dress them up in fantasy, in potential, in hope
Because facing the truth hurts—
and rewriting the story means letting the dream go with it

But red flags don't turn green
not with time, not with patience, not with sacrifice
Love is not meant to wound you in slow, unspoken ways

Let this be the moment
you stop romanticizing inconsistency
and start choosing peace over potential

When the illusion cracks, grief will arrive
not just for the version of them you imagined
but for the version of you who believed
your worth depended on being chosen

Grieving the fantasy is sacred
It is the death of illusion and the return to truth
Let it ache, let it empty you—
because what remains after the grief
is real

Closure Is Something You Choose

Not every heartbreak is loud
Sometimes it's the silence that shatters you

It isn't only the lack of closure that hurts—
it's the confusion, the self-blame,
the way your nervous system keeps replaying
what never resolved

You grieve the potential
the person they might have been
the version of love that almost was

But hear this gently:
an unfinished story doesn't need completion to be closed

You don't need answers or apologies
to reclaim your peace

The silence is your answer
The absence is your clarity
The inconsistency
the unmet needs
the love that kept disappearing—
that is the ending

Closure comes when you stop bargaining with reality
when you stop waiting for someone to choose you differently

You don't need a final conversation to be finished
You can close the door without waiting for someone else
to hand you the key

Sometimes
the only closure
is the choice to stop waiting for one

A Sacred Farewell

A Closure Ritual for Unfinished Stories

This is a ritual of release
A symbolic goodbye for a story that never gave you one

Call forth your willingness to be present
And your quiet courage to let go

Let this be a moment of return
not to the past
but to yourself

You'll need:
– a candle
– a pen and piece of paper
– a fire-safe bowl or dish (optional)

Centre yourself
Light the candle, Sit in stillness
Place one hand on your heart, and the other on your belly
Breathe deeply
Feel yourself arrive fully into this moment

Write
write the name of the person whose presence still lingers in your energy

Beneath it, write:
"I release the story we never finished
I release the hope that kept me waiting
I call my energy back now"

Feel what arises
Let your body speak

Let the ache surface
Let the tears or heat or silence come
There is no wrong way to feel this part

Burn or tear the paper
As the paper turns to ash
or tears into pieces
say aloud:
"I do not need closure to be free
I choose peace
I choose me"

Close the ritual
Blow out the candle
Place both hands over your heart

Whisper softly:
"I am whole
I am free
I am home"

Alchemy of Healing

Perhaps your story does not look exactly like mine
but I know the ache of giving too much
of mistaking sacrifice for love
of not knowing that choosing myself was even an option

What I have learned is this—
healing is not about erasing the past
It is about seeing it differently
I know I have healed when there is no bitterness left in my heart
no ache that keeps circling back
only gratitude for the lessons they taught

The people who could not meet me in the middle
were never the villains of my story
they were mirrors
showing me where I still longed for boundaries,
where my voice was waiting to be claimed,
where my sacred *No* had been abandoned

Every time I chose myself again
the illusion that love lived outside of me dissolved

This is the alchemy of healing—
not pretending the pain didn't pierce
not bypassing the anger
or swallowing the grief
but letting it move through
until it softened into wisdom
expanded into compassion
and carried you into freedom

Sacred Inquiry: Alchemy of Healing

What Was the Lesson?

Take a deep breath, love
Close your eyes and call to mind the version of you who stayed too long—
The one who kept loving in hopes they'd finally see her,
The one who softened her voice, silenced her needs,
and made herself small just to be chosen

Now, ask her gently—not with judgment, but with compassion:
What were you truly seeking?
Was it love... or was it proof that you were someone's first choice?

Let the memories rise
Don't rush to fix them or name them
Simply let them speak

Then ask yourself softly:
–What did that version of me not yet know about her own worth?
–In what ways did I abandon myself to feel safe in someone else?
–What was this relationship trying to teach me, again and again?
–What truth did I finally allow myself to hear when I walked away?

Let your answers come as they wish—quietly, fiercely, or not at all
This is not about reliving the pain
It is about reclaiming the wisdom it left behind

You are not broken because you stayed
But now you are free to love yourself
in the ways you once hoped someone else would

The Invisible Chains of Resentment

Resentment is not just an emotion—
It is an energetic tether

Each time you replay the betrayal,
the abandonment, the confusion,
you send a thread of your life force backward—
tying yourself to the moment it all went wrong
binding yourself to the version of you
who felt powerless, unseen, unloved

When you cling to anger, blame, or sorrow
without letting it move through,
you are not punishing them—
you are punishing yourself
You lock your tenderness in an invisible prison
where the past plays on loop
and the ache becomes identity

Resentment keeps the wound open
Forgiveness, however—
true, embodied forgiveness—
is the key that releases you from the shackles of pain

And that includes the weight you still hold against yourself:
for not leaving sooner
for mistaking pain for passion
for giving too much

You cannot become who you are here to be
while resenting who you once were

Forgiveness is not about who deserves it,
or excusing what happened
It is about who you are becoming
when you choose to release
what was never meant to be carried this long

You are not here to be the warden of your own pain
You are here to rise—
unbound,
untethered,
sovereign

Mini Ritual: The Invisible Chains of Resentment

Untethering from the Past

Find a quiet space where you can be fully with yourself
If you wish, light a candle
Let its flame remind you of the light within you—
steady, eternal, untouched by pain

Close your eyes
One hand rests on your heart
the other on your womb—your centre of power

Breathe slowly, three times
with each exhale, soften further into yourself

Now, bring to mind the person, memory, or wound you are ready to release
See them before you
not as an enemy
but as a soul who once walked beside you

From your heart, golden threads extend
still binding you together
Without force, without blame
begin to call your power back

Whisper:
"Thank you for what you gave me
I honour the role you played in my journey
I honour the lessons it taught
But I no longer want to carry the pain
I call all parts of myself home
I release you now, and I return to me"

In your hands, a golden blade of light begins to form
Pure, compassionate, certain

With love, cut the cord
Watch it dissolve into the earth, into Source
transmuted back into light

Feel the space it leaves behind
Feel your essence gathering—
whole, sovereign, shimmering at your centre
No longer scattered
No longer seeking

Breathe this in
You are free
You are home
It is done

Inner Child & Ancestral Healing

Before the world told you who to be,
you were a girl who was
Whole-hearted, Wide-eyed
Wild with wonder

You found magic in your own company
sang to the sky, spoke to trees,
dreamed aloud without apology

You didn't need to earn love
You were love

But slowly, subtly, the world made you forget
It taught you that belonging required bending
That value had to be gained

You learned to shape-shift
to shine just enough to be safe
to please, to prove, to perform

This is not just about you
Sometimes these threads run older than your body
the ache of generations echoing through your nervous system
ancestral stories woven into your becoming

But now—you remember
You return
You reparent the one within who still believes she must earn
what she already is

She Who Always Knew

She was wonder before she was wounded
she was softness before she was shaped

She spun stories from starlight
danced barefoot in daydreams
spoke her truth before she learned to edit it

She trusted love
she trusted herself

Even after the world carved hesitation into her heart
even after she was told she was too much, too soft, too sensitive
she never stopped knowing that she was enough
that her joy mattered
that her voice had a place

The parts of you that reach and prove and please—they are not flaws
they are the brilliant survival of a little girl
doing her best to stay connected

Now you return to her
not to fix her
not to silence her ache

But to listen with love
to offer her the steadiness the world could not

To remind her
you never stopped being whole
You only forgot for a while

Visualization: She Who Always Knew

The Inner Reunion

Find a quiet space where silence feels like sanctuary
place one hand over your heart, the other over your lower belly
breathe in softly, slowly, deeply

Feel your body settle
feel your soul arrive

Now, close your eyes
and imagine yourself walking down a golden path
each step lighter than the last
each breath drawing you closer to her

Ahead of you
she stands—your younger self
radiant, open, untouched by the noise of becoming

Notice her face, her eyes
how she looks at you

Kneel to meet her where she is
no fixing
no correcting
just being

Gently open your arms and whisper:
"I see you. I hear you. I remember you"

Feel her step into your embrace
feel your arms wrap around her
feel the merging—not as a disappearance
but as a sacred homecoming

Let her light melt into yours
let her wonder reweave itself into your being
let her softness anchor inside your strength

And when you are ready
rise together—
One heart, One voice
whole again

Breathe her in
Let her stay

She is yours—You are hers
And you are home

The Legacy of Lack

Before you ever chased love
you were taught—quietly, insistently
what it was supposed to look like

Maybe you watched the women around you give endlessly
without ever being met in return
Maybe you learned that to be chosen
meant being easy, agreeable, quiet

You heard:
"Be a good girl"
"Be happy with what you were given"
"Love means compromise"

And it wasn't just your household—it was everywhere
Fairy tales, songs, stories that glorified waiting, enduring, sacrificing
This wasn't just **parenting**
It was **programming**

As a child, you absorbed it all
The nervous glance when you asked for too much
The silence when you needed comfort but were told to be strong
The subtle ways love felt conditional—earned rather than given freely

So your little self adapted
She learned to shrink when she felt too big
To please when she longed to protest
To make herself palatable in order to be kept close

Though some of these patterns didn't begin with you
they took root in you

They became the waters your inner child swam in,
the rules she thought she had to obey in order to survive

But what she learned in lack
was never the truth of her worth

The Shift Begins With You

Every time you pause before people-pleasing
you soothe her

Every time you choose rest over rushing to prove your worth
you honour her

Every time you stop chasing what will not choose you
you protect her

Your inner girl is not healed by the perfect partner
She is healed by you—
the safest, softest, most sovereign home she has ever known

You become the love she once waited for
The mother, the advocate, the unwavering presence
she always deserved

Healing is not perfection
It is not the absence of old whispers
It is the building of a sanctuary so steady, so self-honouring
that even when the patterns reappear
you stay rooted

Every return to yourself is a victory
Every act of awareness is a stitch in her mending
You are not starting over when you circle back
You are spiralling inward—
closer and closer
to the truth of who you are

Rewrite Your Inner Script

The path to your authentic self is not about becoming someone new
It is a remembering—
a peeling back of the false lines written over your truth

Before you ever held the pen,
pages were handed to you
filled with roles you never chose,
expectations you never questioned,
beliefs you inherited before you had words

Maybe you were told you were too much—
too emotional, too loud, too soft
So you bent and folded
disappearing into someone else's version of you

But these beliefs are not your truth
They are rehearsals, not reality
Scripts practiced over time—
and just as they were once woven into you,
they can be unwoven, unlearned, rewritten

This is your sacred remembering:
you are not the story someone else wrote
You are the page, yes—
but also the pen and the narrator

You are the living author of a life only you can imagine
And with each choice, each breath, each return to yourself
a new line is written

The Shadows We Inherit

Not every voice in your head is your own
Some took root before you learned the sound of your own voice
Beliefs etched in silence
Patterns passed down like heirlooms

These voices became fluent—so fluent that you mistook them for truth
They told you who to be, how to bend, what to bury
They stitched masks so tightly to your skin, you forgot they weren't yours

But the moment you pause, you hear it—
a quieter voice beneath the noise
The one that asks:
Does this belief expand me or shrink me?
Is this desire born of fear or of love?
If no one else's opinion mattered—what would I choose?

This is not about erasing the past
It is about recognizing what was rehearsed but never real

Authenticity is not found in a single lightning strike of clarity
It is lived in layers
in breath after breath of listening
and choosing

You don't need all the answers to come home
You only need the willingness to hear yourself again
To choose again—
not from fear, not from script, but from sovereignty

Rewriting Through Sacred Choice

Awareness is not the end of the journey
It is the threshold
The doorway into a new way of being

Your patterns are not failures
They are just the echoes of past

But you are no longer bound to them
True empowerment begins in how you choose from here
What once felt like destiny
is now choice

Every time you:
say no without apology
rest without guilt
speak without shrinking
choose love that honours your soul's voice
refuse to chase what was never yours to keep

You liberate

These choices may feel small
but they are sacred sentences,
The architecture of sovereignty

The victory is not in erasing the past
It is in how gently and how fiercely—
you return to your true self

This is authorship in motion—
It is not about perfection,
but about presence

This is the journey back to yourself
And it begins here—
with one conscious choice at a time

Mini Ritual: Choosing Again

Script in the Fire

You will need:
—A Candle
—Paper + pen

Take a blank page
On one side, write the story that is no longer yours—
the belief you inherited
the weight you were never meant to carry

On the other side, write the truth you now choose—
short, alive, in your own words
burning with devotion

Fold the page and place it to your heart
Whisper:
This old story no longer defines me. I choose my truth now

When you are ready, let flame take it—
watch the old dissolve into ash,
watch the new rise in light

Keep the rewritten truth closer to your heart
as a reminder that you are the author now
the pen, the page, the possibility

Soul Blessing

May the stories that no longer serve you
dissolve like ink in water

May your voice rise above the chorus of the past
clear, steady, and wholly your own

And may your pen move with courage and devotion
as you write the story your soul was born to tell

The Mirror That Writes With You

"I am the creator of my own story"

You do not wait for permission
You do not wait to be chosen

Every thought you think is an instruction to the Universe
Every belief you hold is a silent prayer shaping reality

The Universe is not the judge or jury
It does not punish or reward
It only responds—
faithfully, precisely
to the vibration you carry within

It is your sacred co-writer, your mirror
It takes the words you hand it and writes them into form

If you offer a script of fear—scarcity answers
If you embody a story of worthiness—expansion unfolds

This is why rewriting your inner script is sacred work
Not through denial
Not through forced positivity
But through choosing truer words—
words your body can finally trust

Write a reality where you are loved without chasing,
safe without shrinking

And here lies the secret:
the moment you believe you are worthy,
the world reflects it back

Not because it suddenly changed—
but because you finally did

The Spiral Path of Healing

Healing is not a straight line
It is a spiral—
twisting, circling, deepening

Some days you will feel like a goddess—sovereign, magnetic, unshakable
Other days you may shrink again
chase again, forget again

And it can feel devastating
as though all your growth was an illusion

But it isn't
Falling back into old patterns is not failure
It is the nature of the spiral
The difference now is not whether the patterns return
It is how awake you are when they do

There was a time you didn't notice
A time when chasing love still looked like love
A time when you had no tools, no language, no witness within

But now you see
Now you feel
Now you pause

Awareness is proof of your evolution
You are no longer the girl asleep inside the cycle

Even if you fall, you rise faster now
With more softness
more compassion and more wisdom
That's a win worth celebrating

The Threshold of Becoming

You have walked through remembering—
Held the child within to your chest
Listened to the echoes of family and story
Watched false scripts turn to ash in your hands

This was not the birth of someone new
It was the return of someone ancient
The self who never left
only waited beneath the noise
beneath the striving

Now you stand at the threshold of deeper becoming
This next passage is not about searching
It is about alchemy—
The transmutation of wounds into wisdom,
Of insight into essence,
Of worth into embodied power

PHASE 2: THE ALCHEMY WITHIN

She enters the crucible of becoming
No longer awakening from slumber
but stepping into the fire that refines
And choose who she wants to be instead

This is the alchemy within
the unveiling of her hidden essence
the birth of worth as her native tongue
the dance of the goddess in light and dark

Here, she is not performing
She is not proving

She is choosing—
With devotion
with clarity
with love

The Unveiling of Her

There is a version of you
soft yet unshakable
radiant yet rooted—
who moves in rhythm with her own truth

She is not a fantasy
She is your hidden remembrance

Becoming her is not a fabrication
It is a revelation
the shedding of masks—
until what is real rises to the surface

It is not a climb outward
but a gentle falling inward
a homecoming whispered step by step

And you do not have to wait
not for love to arrive
not for the world's permission
not for a sign that you are worthy

The woman you are becoming lives here already
She first arrives in your energy
before she arrives in your life

Each choice becomes devotion
Each gesture becomes a thread
Each detail—however small—
becomes the unveiling of her

You Are the Oracle, Not the Pleaser

You are the channel
not the chaser
You are the medicine
not the martyr
You are the prize
not the persuader

When you remember who you are
You stop offering discounts on your magic
You stop softening your edges to keep others comfortable
You stop translating your truth into a language that dishonours it

Etch this truth into your becoming:
What is meant for me is already mine

You do not beg, perform or prove
You anchor in your own frequency
And from that place—
the people, opportunities, and spaces aligned with you
will arrive with ease

The lighthouse never chases
It shines
It guides
It stands in its own radiance
and lets the world come to it

She Lives in the Details

Begin in whispers, not declarations
Begin in presence, not performance

Your authentic-self lives in the quiet corners
in the way you move through a morning unobserved
in the robe that holds your softness
in the pen that traces your truth across a page

She flickers in the candle you light without reason
in the way your shoulders drop when you feel safe
in the silence you choose over noise
in the dress that makes your soul exhale

These are not small things—They are signals
Each one a note in the song of who you are

She is not summoned by force
She emerges when you honour what feels like home
When you choose the scent that stirs your memory
the book that feeds your becoming
the space that feels like sanctuary

She does not rush
She does not bargain
She simply lives in the details—
awaiting your recognition

Notice her
let these subtleties guide you
She has been with you all along

Glimpse Ritual: She Lives in the Details

Find a quiet space
light a candle if you wish
close your eyes and invite her in—
the woman you are becoming

See her move through her world
Notice the way she dresses herself
not for approval, but for aliveness
the softness of fabric against her skin
the colours that echo her radiance

Sense the quiet devotions of her day
She lingers in the shower as if each drop is baptism
She smooths cream over her body like anointing a goddess
She whispers to her water before she drinks
She pauses to smell the flowers—
not to check a box, but to feel herself come alive

Step into her space
What beauty greets her each day?
What small altars has she placed to her own becoming?
What scents, textures, and colours carry her home to herself?

Now, simply witness her energy
How she stays rooted when the world stirs discomfort
How she breathes instead of abandons herself
How she chooses presence, again and again

You do not need to become her yet
It is enough to glimpse her
to sense her essence living just beneath your skin

Let these details inspire you—
style as soul,
scent as memory,
space as sanctuary,
energy as devotion

From Chasing to Attracting

The magnetic woman
is a mirror of what she desires
She treats herself as the miracle she is—
and the world has no choice but to rise to her frequency

The shift from chasing to attracting begins within
It lives in the beliefs you inherited but never questioned
in the thoughts you repeat without noticing
in the energy you radiate before a single word is spoken

Tend to your inner world until it blooms
Love yourself so wholly you become a reflection for the sacred
Treat your time, your energy, your presence
as holy currency

Becoming magnetic is not about becoming more
It is about becoming true
a return—
to the woman within
who never had to chase
to be worthy of what she seeks

When Worth Becomes Your Native Language

You cannot become the woman you were born to be
while carrying the old script
that taught you to settle for crumbs

Here the story dissolves and a new language takes root
the language of worth
the language of self reverence
the language of radical choosing

Her power is not in her volume
but in her rootedness
in how deeply she listens to her truth

She does not wait to be chosen
she chooses herself
again and again
through ache
through loneliness
through the echo of old stories

It is not her beauty that makes her magnetic
but her embodiment
her unapologetic boundaries
her refusal to betray herself for belonging

To live in this frequency
you must believe you are worthy of it
not someday
now

Self-Worth vs. Self-Value

There is a subtle yet sacred difference between self-worth and self-value
Self-worth is the quiet knowing that you are already enough
unchanged by approval, untouched by achievement, unshaken by opinion

Self-value is how you honour that knowing
in the choices you make
the boundaries you uphold
the places you stay—or walk away from

Worth is belief
Value is embodiment

It sounds like this:
"I am enough as I am—so I will not settle for anything less"
"I am inherently peaceful—so I cut off what drains my tranquillity"
"I deserve to be prioritized—so I no longer chase those who treat me as an option"

You can know you are worthy
and still accept crumbs over a feast
still shrink to be chosen
still overstay in places that erode your light

Why?
Because worth is the root
but value is the bloom

This is your invitation to align the two
to stop knowing in theory and start living in truth

From Potential to Presence

Let people be who they are
Believe them when they show you
Your work is not to fix, wait, or mould someone into readiness
Your work is to see clearly—
to honour what is real, not what you wish it to be

Because potential is not presence
Glimpses are not guarantees
And illusions cannot love you back

When you fall for the maybe, you abandon yourself
You trade devotion to your own becoming
for the fantasy of who they *might* become

But when you choose reality—
You choose you
You choose peace over projection
You choose the sacred ground of what is

The women rooted in her value
No longer mistake intensity for intimacy
No longer betray her peace to keep someone warm

This looks like:
—Slowing down instead of getting swept away
—Listening longer before revealing your soul
—Choosing solitude over confusion
—Asking: Do they meet me in truth, or only in potential?

Walking away from chaos is not a loss
It is a devotion

A vow to your own wholeness
A mirror held to your sacredness

And when you honour what is real,
you clear the way for what is true—
the kind of love, life, and alignment
that never asks you to abandon yourself

Sacred Release: Honouring What's Real

At some point, we all clung to a dream
A version of love that almost fit
A person who almost stayed

Now, it's time to meet yourself with tenderness and ask:
—Where in my past did I confuse potential with presence?
—What has it cost me to wait for someone to become what I needed them to be?
—What does real love feel like in my body?
—What am I no longer willing to compromise in the name of hope?

Let these questions reveal not shame but truth
Let them open the doorway to your becoming

A simple act of release

You will need:
—A candle (white or gold)
—A bowl of water (or natural stream)
—Paper + pen
—A self-worth token (ring, charm, or object that feels sacred to you)

Take a small piece of paper
On one side, write the illusions you carried—
the maybes, the almosts, the promises never kept

On the other side, write your vow to yourself—
the clarity you now choose
the standard you will no longer betray

Place the paper in water

Whisper as it dissolves:
I release the mirage
I return to clarity
I honour what is real

Carry this vow forward
Not as a performance
But as your compass
The quiet song of a woman who no longer waits for potential

No More Discounts on Your Divinity

Healing is devotion
written in breath
lived in choice
embodied in presence

Your standards are not rules for others
They are sacred vows to yourself
The moment you stop undervaluing yourself,
the inherited patterns that bound you
begin to loosen and dissolve

Get clear on who you are becoming
From this moment forward, let your life show the value you claim

Your energy is costly—only those who honour it may enter
Your love is priceless—never to be bargained, never to be begged for
Your heart is sovereign—only those who kneel in reverence may draw near

You are not here to be consumed like a product
Your energy is rare, unrepeatable, and sacred

It is not up for negotiation
It is to be spent, guarded and offered
with exquisite intention

Sacred Boundaries

Boundaries are not punishments
They are permissions—
to rest when you are tired
to walk away when your soul feels small
to remain open only to what expands you

A boundary is not a wall
It is a living threshold
deciding what may cross into your life
and what must remain outside

Every *yes* you give without alignment—
withdraws from your inner account
Every *no* you speak with clarity—
protects your wealth of energy

Boundaries are the quiet mathematics of sovereignty
They are the vault that guards your softness
not a cage, but a temple
where your truth is free to flourish

Practice: Guarding Your Currency

Name the Leak

Think of one place in your life where you feel drained, heavy, or resentful
Ask yourself: *Where am I giving a yes that isn't aligned?*

Rewrite the Exchange

Write down the boundary that would protect your energy in this area
Keep it simple and true, as if you were speaking it to your own heart

Speak the No

Whisper your boundary aloud
Let your body feel the steadiness of it—
not harsh, not defensive
simply clear

Seal the Practice

Place one hand over your heart and one over your belly
Breathe deeply and affirm:
Every no I honour—protects my sacred currency
Every yes I choose—enriches my becoming

Detachment is devotion to self

In this becoming,
detachment is your greatest ally

You do not detach because you no longer care—
you detach because you now choose clarity over illusion
balance over chaos

Detachment is not coldness or withdrawal
it is reverence—
a return to your own rhythm
your own light
your own knowing

It is the refusal to shape-shift for closeness
the refusal to dim your truth for approval
the refusal to bleed for breadcrumbs and call it love

Detachment is not disconnection—
it is sacred reconnection
to your body
to your boundaries
to your worth

The key to higher love is in the quiet strength of letting go
True connection is never born of striving to be chosen
but of choosing yourself so completely
that peace feels more natural than pressure
self-respect feels richer than pursuit

In detachment you still care,
but you no longer cling

You still love,
but you no longer abandon yourself

Detachment whispers:
I trust the timing
I trust the redirection
I trust that what is meant for me will never require me to shrink

And when detachment ripens into practice
it takes form in the way you move
the way you hold yourself steady
the way you protect your softness
without closing your heart

Detachment, Embodied:

Self-possession:

Knowing your worth so deeply that you no longer need to prove it
Remaining anchored in your truth, even when others can't recognize it

Emotional regulation:

No longer outsourcing peace to other people's behaviour
Releasing the need for constant reassurance or validation

Focused presence:

Choosing alignment over chaos
Trusting that what's meant for you will arrive without force
Prioritizing your joy, your vision and your well-being

Sacred boundaries:

You stop making space for energy that dishonours you
You protect your time, your body, your softness—
not out of fear, but out of reverence

Sacred Surrender

Surrender is not giving up
It is the sacred unbinding of what no longer serves you
the gentle choice to trade control for peace

It is the knowing that endings are offerings
and delays are alignments in disguise

Here, you no longer make yourself small
You no longer twist yourself to fit another's longing
You sit back in your worth—
in your softness
in your certainty

And with hands no longer gripping,
you are finally open to receive

Surrender is not an ending
It is a beginning
a widening of the heart to divine rhythm
a willingness to believe life is conspiring in your favour

And from this place of trust, a shift occurs—
You stop seeking love from longing
You begin magnetizing it from overflow

You rest in the knowing:
what is yours will never miss you

Sacred Ritual: Surrender Into Trust

Step 1: Ground Into Presence
Sit or lie down comfortably
Close your eyes
Place one hand over your heart, the other on your belly

Take three deep breaths—inhaling peace, exhaling control
Let your body soften
Let the noise dissolve
Let the now be enough

Step 2: Meet the One Who Clings
In your mind's eye, see her—
the version of you who held on too tightly
who bent herself small to be chosen
who feared letting go because she thought it meant losing love

Walk up to her gently
Hold her hands and whisper:
"You did your best. But you can let go now"
Watch her dissolve into light—released, returned to Source

Step 3: Call Forth the One Who Trusts
Now, see before you the woman you are becoming—
magnetic, serene, anchored in her worth
She no longer chases—she aligns, she receives
She trusts timing, redirection, and divine flow

Invite her to step into you
Feel her merge with your being
Her energy becomes your energy
Her trust becomes your trust

Step 4: Seal With Surrender

Place both hands over your heart and speak aloud:

"I trust the Universe. I trust the flow of life
I trust myself
I no longer chase—I align, I receive, I embody"

Stay here for a few breaths
Let this vibration root itself in your body
When you are ready, open your eyes—anchored, reborn

that calls life to her instead of chasing it away

She is the girl you once were,
now woven into the woman you are becoming
She is the bridge between innocence and sovereignty
A reminder that hope is not naïve—
it is power, when rooted in self-trust

The Inner Maiden is no longer the wound
She is the wellspring
Magnetic, vibrant, alive with her own deservingness

She does not wait for life to choose her
She chooses herself, and in that choice—
she becomes the flame the world cannot look away from

Archetype Embodiment

The Muse, The Mystic & The Queen

As you begin rewriting your inner script
something ancient stirs awake
These are not roles to strive toward—
they are archetypal frequencies encoded in your bones
your breath
your becoming

They live in you
They wait for you
They rise the moment you choose to live as the main character of your life

The Muse—She Who Dances in Her Own Light

The Muse does not wait to be seen
She is a living canvas—art in motion, beauty in devotion
She wears colour like truth
She moves as though life itself is a love story worth savouring

She reminds you:
"You are allowed to be both the masterpiece and the artist"

Call on her when:
—You need to remember your natural magnetism
—You are ready to stop chasing and start *inviting*
—You long to romanticize your life
especially the quiet, unnoticed moments

The Mystic—She Who Trusts the Unseen

The Mystic listens inward before she moves outward
She co-creates with the unseen, honours divine timing, and walks in prayer with every step
Her truth is whispered—but thunderously known

She whispers:
"You are not just a woman. You are the vision and the vessel"

Call on her when:
—You are alchemizing fear into faith
—You are anchoring into spiritual truth through affirmations, ritual, or intuitive practice

—You are surrendering the timeline and choosing trust

The Queen—She Who Anchors in Worth

The Queen does not perform
She presides
She commands not through force, but through embodied presence
Her worth is unquestionable
Her boundaries are sacred ground

She declares:
"My presence is the standard
My life is the kingdom
I do not beg—I create"

Call on her when:
—You feel the urge to shrink, compromise, or perform for love
—You need to remember your value is not up for negotiation
—You are reclaiming your relationship with power, peace, and devotion to self

A Note on Archetypes

These are not distant myths
They are mirrors—radiant reflections of what already lives within you
When you write a new story, you are not just healing the past
You are awakening the full spectrum of your feminine power

You are no longer a side character in someone else's script
You are the sacred author
You are the pulse, the pen, the page

And the story you write now
Is worthy of your own awe

Daily Archetypal Invocation

If you wish to deepen your connection to these energies each day, you may speak this simple invocation aloud or silently:

"Today I walk in radiance, like the Muse

I trust the unseen, like the Mystic

I claim my worth, like the Queen

And I live as the sacred author of my life"

Breathe it in
Let it settle into your bones
Even a whispered sentence carries the power to reshape your reality

The Dance of the Goddess

She is both flame and stillness—
the wild rose and the rooted oak

She does not chase
She magnetizes, alchemizes and becomes

This is the dance of the balanced feminine—
where softness and strength are no longer at war,
but move in a sacred rhythm

This is the return to your feminine temple

Reclaiming the Forgotten Power

For so many of us, the world conditioned us to survive in our masculine
We learned to strive, to plan, to protect, to push
We were praised for our productivity, resilience, and independence—
but rarely for our softness, our stillness, or our sensitivity

And so, we forgot
We forgot that we are both
Feminine and masculine
Two rivers meant to flow in balance

To remember is to reclaim the power of presence—
our capacity to feel, to receive and to simply be

And in that remembering, the full spectrum of the feminine returns
The softness and the fire
The nurturing and the knowing
The Divine and the Dark

This is not about abandoning the masculine
He is sacred too—clarity, structure, action, protection
But he was never meant to stand alone
Only when both are honoured
Do we rise whole

So we begin here
Not by rejecting one
But by reclaiming the part we left behind
Allowing her fullness to flow again

The Light Within

Radiance, Grace & Sacred Flow

The Divine Feminine is light embodied—
a living current of grace, love, and creation
She is the goddess within you—serene, sensual, sovereign
She doesn't hustle to prove her value
She knows it
And from that knowing, she becomes magnetic

She trusts the unfolding
She honours her intuition
She lives in harmony with the rhythms of life, not in resistance to them

To embody her is to soften into life
while standing rooted in your truth
It is feeling so safe in your own skin
that you no longer chase love, approval, or belonging
You magnetize instead of pursue
You receive instead of reach

Begin here—
not with strategy, but with devotion

Presence Over Pace

Slow your breath
Soften your body
Take your time dressing, eating, arriving
The feminine is never in a rush
She is a ceremony of now

Pleasure as Compass

Pleasure is not just sensual
It is sensory
Let texture awaken you
Let scent stir your memory
Let beauty interrupt your day
Ask not what is productive—
but what is alive for me right now?

Lead with Feeling, Not Logic

The Divine Feminine trusts the flutter in her belly
the pull in her chest
She does not demand proof
She follows resonance
Ask yourself:
What feels true?
What feels soft?
Where does my body lean forward without fear?

Receive Without Earning

Let love land
Let praise stay
Let rest be sacred
Let abundance meet you without apology
You don't have to work for what your soul already deserves

When you return to your Divine Feminine
you become a sanctuary for your own heart
You move with grace, not urgency
You soften like dusk meeting the sea
You open—
and you allow

And from that sacred stillness
life begins to pour into you
Not because you fought for it
but because you finally
made space for it

The Shadow Queen

Sovereignty, Boundaries & Sacred Fire

If the Divine Feminine is radiant moonlight,
the Dark Feminine is the starless sky—
mysterious, primal, and equally sacred

She is the quiet before the storm
the whisper that says, *no more*
She is the sacred disruptor
the keeper of thresholds
the woman who remembers her power even in the dark

She is the Black Cat, the Witch, the Siren
Unbothered
Unapologetic
Unavailable for anything less than truth

She does not chase
She does not explain
She chooses herself—
even if it means being misunderstood

She is the wild feminine—
the version of you who protects her energy like holy ground

To embody the Dark Feminine
is to rise as your own protector—
to become the temple, the doorway, the flame that guards it

Honour Your No

No is a spell, a shield, a complete sentence

Discomfort is enough
If your body withdraws, so do you
The Shadow Queen does not betray herself for approval

See Without Illusion

Fantasy is not love—it is longing in disguise
She takes off the rose-coloured lenses
She lets people reveal themselves
and believes them the first time

Refuse the Cage of "Too Much"

She is not too wild, too deep, too intense
She is simply not for shallow waters
Those who fear your truth will always call it excess
Let them go
Keep your fire

Choose Sovereignty Over Nostalgia

Even when it aches
Even when the past calls in a familiar voice
She does not crawl back to cages she has burned down
She chooses her future over her history

She reminds you:
Your silence is a boundary
Your absence is a mirror
Your energy is not owed

You are the altar and the flame
the sovereign and the spell
the queen who does not ask permission—
she simply reigns

The Sacred Union of Divine Grace & Dark Sovereignty

To live in your feminine power
is to carry the softness of the Divine
and the strength of the Dark

To be both the gentle tide and the crashing wave
the muse and the mirror
the nurturer and the storm
the holy water and the wildfire

When these currents meet in harmony
something ancient stirs within you
You become unshakable
You stop over giving and start receiving
You stop proving and start embodying
You stop chasing and start magnetizing

The truth is—
wholeness is not a destination
It is a frequency

Some days you will resist
Some days you will forget

But the vow remains:
to rise again and again
until softness feels like strength
until stillness feels safe
until boundaries feel like grace

This is not a performance
It is a homecoming
Messy
Nonlinear
Holy in its unfolding

Sacred Practice: Listening to the Body's Yes and No

Your body speaks in sensation
Her language is not logic, but feelings

To learn her voice
you must practice listening

The Ritual

Create Space
Find a quiet room where you will not be disturbed
Dim the lights, light a candle if you wish
Place one hand over your heart, one hand over your womb

Anchor With Breath
Close your eyes and take three slow, steady breaths
Imagine inhaling safety, exhaling tension
Let your body soften into presence

Ask a Gentle Question
Whisper to yourself: *Body, show me my Yes*
Wait for a response—not in your mind, but in sensation

Notice
Do you feel warmth? Expansion? A softening of the chest or belly? A sense of openness?
Sit with it for a few breaths

Ask Again
Now whisper: *Body, show me my No*

Notice
Do you feel constriction? Tightness? A pulling back? A heaviness in the chest or

throat?

Trust whatever arises

Seal the Dialogue

Thank your body for speaking

Whisper

I will honour your wisdom. I will not abandon your voice

Rooted in Her Own Rhythm

This path is not about passivity
It is about devotion
It is about moving through the world with such reverence for your own truth
that you no longer abandon yourself
for love
for comfort
for approval

To live rooted in your own rhythm
is to remember that your body sets the tempo
not the demands of others
not the noise of the world

It is a slow exhale that cannot be rushed
a soft yes that needs no justification
a quiet knowing that whispers
I am already enough

Feminine energy reminds you
if something costs your peace, your softness, or your self-worth—
it is far too expensive

You are not here to contort
You are meant to live in a way that feels like home in your bones

And as you return to this rhythm, you'll notice—
life begins to move with you

The right people find your pace
Opportunities arrive in divine timing
Your days stop feeling like a chase
and start flowing like a dance

The essence of feminine power
is the alignment so deep
that the world adjusts to meet you

Here, you are not waiting for permission
You are not proving your worth
You are simply living as yourself

And in that living
you create coherence—
inside and out

Let this be your vow:
to walk to the beat of your own becoming
to soften where you once braced
to rise where you once shrank
to choose what feels true over what looks acceptable

Because when you are rooted in your own rhythm
you no longer fear losing love by being yourself
You know, with every breath,
that the deepest love you could ever need
begins within

Sacred Reflection: The Feminine Path Home

You've reclaimed pieces you once left behind
You've met both your radiance and your shadow
You've remembered that your rhythm is enough

Now let it land

Close your eyes
Place one hand on your heart, the other on your womb space
Breathe into the quiet between beats
Notice—
without fixing
without forcing
what stirs within you

Whisper to yourself:
I am safe to live as I am

Then ask:
—Who am I when I no longer betray myself for approval?
—What does wholeness feel like in my body—not as perfection, but as presence?
—How does life move when I let my rhythm lead?

Let the answers rise like tidewater—
slow, sacred and certain

When you're ready, write down one truth that surfaced
Carry it forward as a vow, a compass, a reminder

This is the beginning of your embodiment
A homecoming to the woman you were always meant to be

Now, She Embodies

She has chosen
Not just who she is
but who she refuses to be

The old names no longer fit
The old roles no longer cling
Her skin remembers the shedding

This is the crossing
from decision to embodiment
from choosing in silence
to living in motion

She no longer speaks of change
She carries it in her breath
in her walk
in the way her eyes meet the world

No more rehearsals
No more shadows of almost
Only the rhythm of a woman who knows
that her truth is not an idea
but a living pulse within her

PHASE 3: THE DIVINE EMBODIMENT

She moves with intention
With intuition
With an inner rhythm no one else needs to understand

In this sacred return to the body
Now you begin to live the frequency of your truth

Not by chasing, but by aligning
Not by force, but by flow

You become magnetic—not because you seek to be seen,
but because you have finally chosen to see yourself

She Is You, Remembered

You have taken off the masks you didn't even know you wore
You've awakened the sacred currents within you
And now you stand on holy ground—
A clean slate,
An open vessel for truth

How you move now
How you embody this frequency
Will make all the difference

She is not a fantasy
Not a disguise
Not an unreachable ideal

She is the stillness that hums in your chest
when you no longer beg for belonging
The grace behind your silence
The holiness in your boundaries
The softness within your surrender

She is the woman who no longer explains her worth
or bargains with her knowing
or stays where her soul withers

She moves slowly, deliberately—
as if dancing with time itself

She is truth, embodied
A mirror of your worth
Reflected in the choices you make
when no one is watching

To walk as Her
To choose alignment over effort
Presence over performance

To ask again and again:
What does love for myself look like today?
What version of me emerges when I trust instead of grasp?
How can I honour Her in this breath, in this step?

She is not someone you become
She is someone you remember
And now—
She takes the lead

The Subtle Rhythms of Self-Devotion

She does not need ten tasks before sunrise to feel worthy
She meets herself daily in quiet ways that whisper
I love you
I've got you
I will not abandon you

Rituals are not chores
they are sacred pauses—anchors of remembrance

A woman who knows her worth does not perform only when eyes are on her
Her rituals are private offerings—acts of devotion without an audience

She might
pour her tea slowly and sip in silence
write her desires not just her doubts
dress for the goddess she is even when no one will see
speak to her reflection with tenderness not critique
say no without apology
say yes with her whole body

These are not habits
they are affirmations in motion
Each choice a vow

When you live in the rhythm of your worth
life begins to echo it back
People treat you the way you treat yourself
Opportunities arrive at the frequency of your self-regard
You no longer entertain crumbs
because you have tasted your own abundance

Embodiment Practice

The Subtle Rhythms of Self-Devotion

Choose one simple act today
brushing your hair
pouring tea
walking barefoot on the earth

Meet it without distraction
without hurry
without needing to be anywhere else

Let your breath guide you
your senses awaken
Let this moment hold you

This is how you return
to the holy within the habitual
to devotion woven through the everyday
to living inside your life instead of moving past it

Grace in Motion

She moves with storms not against them
a soft flame in the winds of change

Grace is the power woven through stillness
a quiet defiance in a world addicted to noise

To walk as Her is not to bypass emotion
but to feel so deeply, wholly, fiercely

She does not suppress what rises
She breathes through it
listens without being led by it
She lets it move through her—
but never dictate her direction

This is grace in motion
to stay rooted while the winds howl
to remain soft without collapsing
to move forward without forcing

Grace begins within the body
Your breath is the anchor
your boundaries the sacred lines
your nervous system the compass that returns you home

To be Her is not to never wobble
but to meet yourself when you do
to pause instead of crumble
to breathe instead of flee
to choose your response instead of leaking power

This is self-regulation
the art of presence without performance
the sovereignty of energy that does not beg to be seen

She does not rush to prove or explain
She does not shrink to keep the peace

Her stillness sharpens her
Her energy speaks without raising her voice

This is feminine power embodied
not loud but undeniable
not rigid but unshakable
a woman who remembers she is the calm in the storm

Your Body Always Knows

Your body is your oracle
Your sacred truth-teller

She speaks long before the mind can find words
She speaks in whispers—
a flutter in the belly
a tightening in the chest
a subtle pull toward or away

She speaks through breath that catches
hands that tremble
shoulders that rise before a word escapes your lips

This is intuition—
Not fantasy
Not fear
but the quiet knowing that lives in your feminine core

When you feel contraction, she is saying *pause*
When you feel expansion, she is saying *proceed*
Your body doesn't argue
She reveals

And yet—
when life shakes you
when love cracks you open too wide, too soon
your nervous system may close its doors
You may feel numb

This is not betrayal
It is protection
A sacred "not yet" whispered by the body that keeps you safe

In those moments, self-devotion becomes your medicine
Breathe deeper than the story
Lay your hand over your heart and whisper, *I am safe now*
Touch your skin as if greeting an old friend
Rock yourself back into rhythm until the trembling subsides

Then—return to listening
Because your body is never wrong
She remembers what the mind forgets
She will always guide you home
You only have to slow down enough to hear her

Embodiment Practice: Coming Home to Grace

The next time you feel unsteady
when your body is heavy or tense
when the mind spirals and the world grows too loud

Pause
Place one hand on your heart
one on your belly
Close your eyes

Inhale for four counts
Hold for four
Exhale for six

Whisper softly
It is safe to stay with me
It is safe to pause
Repeat until your body begins to soften

Then listen
Does she need rest
a nap in the middle of the day
to sit beneath the sky
to cry without explanation
to feel without fixing

Take all the time you need
Be generous with yourself
Let the moment be your compass
Let your body lead you home

And when you return to centre
Ask gently:

—Where am I still moving from fear
from the ache of abandonment
from the hunger to be seen

—If I chose grace over urgency, what would soften in me?

—How would life unfold
if I moved with presence rather than pressure?

Wholeness as Your Baseline

She no longer climbs ladders that lead her away from her soul
She no longer measures her worth in numbers, followers, or flawless days

Her success is quieter now—
it lives in the way her shoulders soften at sunset
in the way her boundaries speak both "yes" and "no" with grace

It's in the joy that rises without reason
the stillness that whispers:
You are not late
not lacking
not behind

She no longer seeks to be filled—
she is already brimming
Not from what she has gathered,
but from what she has remembered

Her wholeness isn't something she found—
it's something she returned to

Anchored in Alignment

Society sold us a blueprint of the “high-value woman”—
impeccably independent
flawlessly composed
always producing, always proving

We were taught that value is earned through performance—
through the right body, the right brand, the right hustle

But that version is curated, conditional, exhausting
When you unravel what isn’t truly yours
you stop moving from lack
and start living from alignment

Wholeness is not about fitting an image
it’s about living as you are—
softer, slower, bolder, quieter, messier
than the world may expect

She no longer edits herself to be digestible
She lets go of what no longer aligns, even if it once felt familiar
She doesn’t hustle for validation
She anchors into self-trust

Because in overflow, nothing is forced
and nothing meant for you can be lost

The Language of Overflow

You give without resentment
You receive without guilt

You no longer over-explain
Over-apologize
Or over-perform for crumbs

You radiate ease, even when life is not easy
You discern instead of tolerate
You rest without guilt

You celebrate your enoughness without needing an audience
You stop asking, "Am I too much?"
and start asking, "Is this enough for me?"

Sacred Inquiry: Anchored in Enoughness

Take a slow, gentle breath
Soften into the truth of this moment
Let the layers fall—the ones you wore to be worthy

Now ask yourself...

- Where have I been bending to fit an image of "value" that was never mine?
- What parts of me have I silenced, polished, or shrunk to be palatable?
- Where have I abandoned ease for approval, moving from fear or scarcity instead of trust?
- If I truly believed I was already whole—already worthy—what would I stop chasing?
- What does overflow feel like in my body right now—in my breath, my choices, my pace?
- How would it change the way I give and receive, if I offered only from fullness, never depletion?

Let these truths land softly in your heart:
Your worth is not a performance
It is a presence
And from that presence, you overflow—effortlessly, endlessly

The Open-Hearted Yes

She smiles and simply says, thank you
No flinching
No shrinking
No offering it back to stay small

Once, strength looked like self-denial
Now, strength is letting love land

To receive without apology—
to let compliments settle into the body
to welcome support without guilt or performance—
this is a return to your feminine essence

There is quiet power in openness
There is radiance in your yes
You do not need to match or prove or explain
Your only task is to breathe into your heart
and let yourself be adorned by life

Control once felt like safety
Gripping, bracing, planning
So you wouldn't fall

Now, safety is surrender—
not collapse, but power redefined
It is opening the fists that once clenched in fear
It is whispering, I trust life to meet me where I am

The Subtle Art of Allowing

There was a time when kindness unsettled me
A coffee offered, a compliment spoken, a hand reaching out—
and my instinct was to even the scale
"I'll get the next one," I'd reply,
not from generosity, but from a quiet unease of owing

Beneath those small gestures lived a deep belief:
ease must be earned, support must be matched
To accept freely was indulgent, unfair, unsafe

But that is not the truth
That is survival logic, not soul logic
An old wound dressed as virtue

Now, I see the grace in allowing myself to be held
Not as debt, but as love
Not as imbalance, but as belonging

Ease is not laziness
Provision is not weakness
Receiving is not shameful
It is the natural beat of love

The more I allow myself to be held—
by people, by the Universe, by love itself—
the more I learn that balance was never about keeping score
It was about harmony

You are safe to lean
Safe to soften
Safe to let it be easier

Sacred Invitation: The Chalice of Receiving

Find a quiet, nourishing space
Light a single candle before you
Let its flame remind you of the light you carry within

Close your eyes
Place one hand on your heart, one on your womb

Breathe slowly, deeply
Let each inhale open you
Let each exhale release what is no longer needed

Now, envision a golden chalice resting at the centre of your chest
This chalice is your essence—
your inner spring of worthiness and light
With every breath, watch it fill

Inhale: trust, radiance, wholeness
Exhale: scarcity, doubt, the old chase

Whisper softly into the flame:
" I *am open to receive. I trust the flow of my journey*"

Repeat until the words hum through your body like a prayer
Feel the golden light overflowing from your heart
spilling through your body, your breath, your being
It touches everything you are and everything you offer

You are not pouring from emptiness
You are already full
You are the gift
You are the source

When you are ready, return gently
knowing this chalice within you is always here
and this flame of receptivity is yours to tend

The Anchor and the Ocean

You have remembered your wholeness
You have softened into the art of receiving
Now you arrive at another threshold—
not only the fullness of the feminine
but the balance of both energies within you

The feminine and masculine are not opposites
They are companions, meant to move in harmony
Your softness will not diminish by structure
Your structure will not collapse by tenderness

You are not only the river,
but also the banks that guide its flow
You are not only the ocean,
but the anchor that steadies its vastness

This is the place of inner union
where receptivity finds safety in presence
and presence finds purpose in devotion
Here, you remember—
you were never just one side of the whole
You are both
And together, they make you unshakable

The Union of Yin and Yang

There is a quiet dance unfolding inside you
A rhythm to be remembered

They are the yin and yang of your inner world
Two sacred poles within your psyche
meant to move in balance

The inner feminine is your flow—
your intuition, your feeling, your cyclical wisdom
She creates, nurtures, softens, and receives
She is the moon that waxes and wanes with mystery

The inner masculine is your clarity—
your grounded presence, your structure
He acts, protects, builds, and sustains
He is the sun that rises each day without fail

You need both
The feminine calls you inward,
the masculine helps you move outward
The feminine dreams,
the masculine builds what she imagines
The feminine surrenders,
the masculine steadies her trust

Union is not about perfection
It is about listening—
knowing when to rest
and when to rise
when to feel
and when to act

This is the sacred polarity within you
Not dominance or division
but harmony embodied

Sacred Integration: The Dance Within

Find a quiet moment
Let your breath soften the edges of this day
Feel both the stillness and the stir of life within you

When your inner feminine drifts without anchor
she waits, aches, longs to be chosen

When your inner masculine is wounded
he silences, he controls, he mistakes force for safety

But when they meet in reverence—
you rise unstoppable
You lead with grace
You surrender with discernment
You rest without guilt
You act without rushing

Now, gently ask yourself
—Where am I leaning too far into softness
without offering myself structure?

—Where am I moving from force
instead of clarity and care?

—Do I feel safe within myself to be both held and free?

—What does harmony feel like in my body
when my feminine and masculine move as one?

Breathe into the answer that arises
Let it ripple through your chest, your belly, your bones

And carry this whisper with you—
I am both
the one who feels and the one who protects the feeling
the softness and the steel
I am led by my own clarity
and held by my own arms
I am already whole

The Flame and the Field

There is a stillness in a woman who knows her worth
She becomes a quiet current that draws the world in without effort

This is not about performance or manipulation
Not about being hard to get or turning herself into a spectacle
It's about being so rooted in essence, so aligned with truth
that what's meant for her gravitates toward her—effortlessly

When she no longer clings to outcomes or timelines
When she no longer auditions for belonging or overexplains her worth
something shifts
Scarcity dissolves

She radiates ease, trust, joy, and self-honoring
She no longer convinces—she invites
Through her presence, her softness, her luminous self-respect

Magnetism is not in how she looks
but in how she feels
Grounded, intentional, embodied

Her worth does not spike when praised or shrink when questioned
It lives in her walk, her voice, her gaze
It breathes in her discernment—choosing peace over chaos
Her joy is quiet but undeniable
Her aliveness warm and unshakable

Magnetism isn't something she turns on
It's who she becomes when she no longer abandons herself

Power Draped in Silk

Power is not always a roar
Sometimes it is the pause before she speaks
The stillness in her gaze that says, *I know who I am*

She no longer clamours to be understood
She no longer outsources her voice to approval
Her silence can land heavier than performance ever could

Soft power is choosing your energy as carefully as silk—
for how it feels against the skin of your soul
not for how the world perceives it

It is the paradox of being both spine and surrender
warmth and wildness
tenderness and unshakable truth

When you walk with a strong back and an open heart
you become a quiet revolution
Boundaries turn into silk-wrapped steel—
soft to the touch, unbreakable at the core
Your "no" becomes a devotion, not a defence
Your "yes" a holy offering

This is the sacred duality of the feminine
Her mystery is not invitation—it is discernment
Her softness is not weakness—it is grace choosing its ground
Her presence speaks what words cannot
A spell woven in breath, silence, and sovereign ease

The Silent Power of Energy

You do not have to explain your worth
you do not have to defend your standards
your energy speaks for you

It shows in the way you walk away without bitterness
in the way you choose peace without explanation

This is not coldness
it is clarity
it is knowing your presence is a temple
and not every soul is meant to enter

Your standards are your silent teachers
your embodiment the loudest truth
You teach others how to treat you
by how you treat yourself

Stand before a mirror
look into your own eyes
and speak like you mean it

I am no longer available for what waters me down
I am the lead of my own story

Say it until your bones remember
until your posture shifts
until your silence carries your truth

When your energy shifts
your reality follows
not by force
but by frequency

Integration: The Silk Flame

Sacred Inquiry

Where in your life do you shine too brightly for approval rather than from truth? Where do you soften to please, instead of softening from strength?

Practice

Light a Candle
Place it before you as a symbol of your flame
Watch its radiance—steady, magnetic, unforced
Let it remind you: your energy attracts without reaching

Wrap in Silk
Take a scarf, shawl, or even a blanket
Drape it gently across your shoulders
Feel its softness as both comfort and boundary
Whisper to yourself:
"My softness is sovereign. My presence is enough"

Anchor the Duality
Close your eyes
Breathe into your heart as you imagine both flame and silk within you:
– Flame: your radiance, your truth, your warmth
– Silk: your discernment, your boundaries, your grace

Let them meet
Strong spine, open heart
Unshakable, yet tender

Reflection

Journal on this

—What shifts when I embody both flame and silk?
—How does it change the way I give my energy?
—How does it change the way I receive?

Dance Like She's Watching

She is watching—
not with judgment,
but with awe

The woman you are becoming
witnesses you now

She smiles
when you touch your skin with reverence
She softens
when you let rhythm move through you
She rises
every time you choose love over shame

This is not for the world's gaze
This is for Her—
the one within you
the one you are returning to

Move for her
Dress for her
Dance for her

She's watching—
and she remembers
You were always this remarkable

Your Flesh Is Scripture

Your body is not separate from your healing
This body—soft, fierce, aching, alive—
is the altar

She remembers everything you've tried to forget
and longs to be held with reverence

This avatar is the temple of your becoming
the vessel through which your soul experiences form
Your curves, your scars, your stretch marks—
they are not flaws
but scripture written in flesh

Care for this vessel
Nourish it, strengthen it, let it rest
but let love be your devotion
not fear or false idols

Embodiment Practice: The Temple of You

This is not about perfecting your body
It is about coming home to it
Honouring the vessel that carries your soul with reverence

What you'll need:

- A quiet space where you won't be disturbed
- Loose clothing or lingerie that makes you feel free and alive
- A playlist that awakens something soft and slow within you
- Optional: a favourite oil, lotion, or fragrance

Begin:
Set your space
Light a candle
Let the music slow your breath, loosen your edges
Let the air itself feel sacred

Dress in a way that delights your own skin—as though preparing for a lover
Only this time the lover is you

Now touch your body
Not with critique, not with demand—but with awe

Trace the lines of your arms, your collarbone, your waist
Run your hands through your hair as though it were silk spun for you alone
Feel your skin—its warmth
Its aliveness

Let it remind you
This body is not a project
It is a temple

Let movement rise from sensation
Sway, roll your hips, close your eyes
Don't perform—listen
Let your body lead, let your hands follow

Whisper inward:
I am safe in my body
This vessel is sacred
I choose to treat her with love

This is not performance
This is prayer made flesh

Sacred Inquiry: Meeting the Edge

Your body has been with you through it all
She held you through heartbreak
She carried you when you felt too heavy
She softened when joy finally returned

Now pause and ask gently:
—What awakens in me when I let myself feel sensual—just for me?

—Where does resistance live—
in my breath, my belly, my gaze?

—What unspoken rules am I still holding
about what beauty should look like?

—If I saw my body as holy,
how would I touch her, feed her, move her, dress her?

Let this not be measurement but mirror—
a mirror that shows you how sacred she always was

Fall in love with your body
not because of how she looks
but because she is you

This vessel
This sacred vessel
The temple you were entrusted with
The only love and acceptance she ever needed
was yours

Mantra: This Body, This Blessing

This sacred vessel—I cherish her
There is only one of me in the entire universe

I was never meant to look like anyone else
I was always meant to look like me

I nourish her with love
I move her with devotion

I am a miracle in motion
I am sacred
I am whole
I am enough

Walking With Devotion

She no longer moves with urgency
She moves with reverence
Not because she has nowhere to be—
but because she is exactly where she is supposed to be

Her life has become her holy ground
Every breath, every gesture, every ordinary act—
a quiet offering of love to the self within

To romanticize your life is not to decorate it for display
It is not a performance for the eyes of others
It is an intimacy with yourself
a way of moving through the day as though the mundane is already sacred

This isn't pretence
It's noticing
Noticing the weight of your inhale and the sweetness of your exhale
The warmth of sunlight across your collarbone
The hush between one heartbeat and the next

It is remembering that beauty begins in your awareness
not in perfection
That your presence is the poetry
That your being is the art

To romanticize your life is to live as if you are the muse
Because you are

Living as a Love Poem

Everyday Altars

Begin your mornings like a slow kiss
as if greeting a beloved—Because you are
You're greeting yourself

Sip something warm
Let music soften the silence
Meet your own gaze in the mirror
not to fix—but to feel
Ask yourself, gently:
How do I want to feel today?

Let your space whisper love
You don't need a shrine
just intention
—a flower by your bed
—a stone that feels like memory
—a handwritten note that says:
You are **held**

Whatever reminds you that this life is yours
Choose that

Make the mundane magical
You are not doing chores
You are tending to your temple

Add rose oil to your laundry
Hum to the rhythm of your stirring spoon

Let the wind kiss your neckline when you walk
Let your life flirt with you

Dress like the goddess within is watching
Not to impress
but to express

Soft fabrics that ask to be touched
Colours that speak your mood out loud
Getting dressed becomes devotion—not duty

What makes you feel most *you*?
Start there

Nourish yourself like it's a prayer
Feeding your body is feeding your soul
Even if it's just you and the quiet
Light a candle
Say thank you
Taste slowly
Let every bite be an offering

Write love letters to yourself
Become your own admirer
Start with:
Dear me, I see you. I love you
Let it be messy, tender, real
Let your pen become a mirror for your heart

Pause like it's sacred
Life moves fast
but you don't have to

Close your eyes
Place a hand over your heart

Ask:
What do I need right now?
And then listen

Sacred living begins here—
in small, quiet choices that honour your aliveness
Your life can be a love poem
written one moment at a time

Guarding the Garden

Now you've become untouchable to chaos
You've grown roots deep into the soil of your own worth
Unapologetically, unwaveringly, fully choosing yourself

This choice has built a sanctuary inside you
not to hide, but to tend what matters most

Being unavailable to what no longer aligns is not closing off
It is choosing where your energy flows
It is devotion in action

You still love deeply
You still show up for those who nourish you
But not everyone receives a key to your sanctuary

You begin to ask of each invitation:
Does this feel safe for my nervous system
Does this feed my soul or simply distract it
Is this aligned with the woman I am becoming

You learn the difference
between a soul-yes and a self-abandonment
and that knowing becomes your compass

You pour your attention like holy water
only where it is sacred
only where it is met with reverence

Your softness is not for convincing
It is a gift
a prayer
a boundary of tenderness

So you guard the garden gently
let your edges be careful and kind
let your yes be spacious and sacred
let your no be simple and true

You are the keeper of your temple
and tending it is your devotion to yourself

Integration: Tending the Inner Garden

Find a quiet space where you can be alone with yourself
Light a candle or place a small object before you—
something that feels like an emblem of beauty, devotion, or peace

Close your eyes
Breathe slowly into your body
Feel your roots extending down into the earth, anchoring you in the soil of your own worth

Place one hand on your heart and the other on your belly
Whisper gently to yourself:
I am the keeper of my garden
My energy is holy

Now imagine the sanctuary within you—
a lush, blooming inner garden that only you can tend
See its colours, feel its textures, notice the fragrance of its flowers
Notice the gates—that protect it
yet gentle—strong

With each breath, picture yourself watering the soil with love
Removing what no longer belongs
Allowing space for what nourishes you to grow

When you are ready, open your eyes and write down three truths:

What am I saying no to?
What am I saying yes to?
How I will guard this garden with love, not fear?

Keep these words somewhere close—
a reminder of the devotion to your becoming

The Soft Revolution

She didn't arrive here by accident
She became this version of herself on purpose—
By choosing softness when it would've been easier to shut down
By choosing grace when the world cornered her to harden
By choosing truth over perfection
Presence over performance
Embodiment over applause

This is not a return to an outdated idea of womanhood
It is a reclamation—
a rebirth into a new feminine paradigm
One that is soul-led
self-honouring
and unapologetically whole

You are not who you were when this phase began
You are softer now—and therefore stronger
You move slower—and therefore with deeper power
You speak less—and yet your energy echoes louder

You are the quiet revolution
The soft storm
The woman who leads with grace
and commands without force

Let yourself honour this becoming
You are no longer reaching for her
You are walking as her now

In the Wake of Her Bloom

This is not just a pause
It is a consecration
A sacred breath between chapters
A moment to honour the soft storm you are—
To celebrate the woman who rose,
who remembered,
who returned to herself

You Will Need:

- A candle (any colour that feels sacred to you)
- A small bowl of water
- A mirror
- A symbol of your feminine essence—a silk scarf, a flower, a piece of jewellery... whatever whispers you

The Ritual

Create Your Altar
Gather your items with care
Light the candle
Place the mirror before you
Let the flame reflect your inner fire
Let the water hold your softness
This is your altar—an offering to your becoming

Anoint and Reflect
Dip your fingertips in the water
Touch your forehead, your heart, your womb—

And whisper with each:
"I honour the wisdom of my mind"
"I honour the truth of my heart"
"I honour the power of my womb—my source, my knowing, my creation"

Now look into the mirror—
not to fix
not to critique
But to truly see

See the woman who grieved, who grew
Who softened and stood again
Let her know she is seen
She is sacred
She is home

Wear Your Symbol
Hold your chosen item close
Or place it upon your body with reverence
Then speak:
"I love being a woman
I am the keeper of tenderness
and the holder of storm
I am the wildfire
and the holy water

My softness is not small
My power is not loud
I lead with presence
I live with poetry
I am not becoming...
I already am"

Final Blessing

Place both hands over your heart
Close your eyes
Take a long, slow breath in
And as you exhale, let this prayer move through you

May I walk forward with devotion, not urgency
May I remember that power can be silent and still
May I trust the wisdom in my body
The rhythm in my breath
The universe within me
And the love that brought me here

After the Becoming

This next path is not about becoming more
It is about staying true
when the noise grows loud
when the world forgets what she now knows

It is about choosing alignment
over urgency
devotion over distraction
trust over fear

Welcome to Phase Four
The Eternal Alignment
Where her anchor is not the world outside
but the truth she embodies within
Where she learns to live not just as herself—
but as the soul she has always been

Phase 4: The Eternal Alignment

You have already shed the skins that were never yours
You have rewritten the scripts handed down through silence and survival
You have stepped into a life that feels aligned with your truest nature

Now comes the sacred task of remaining
Of living as her—not only when the world affirms your becoming
but also when the external wavers, resists, or does not yet reflect your truth

This phase is not about more fixing, more striving or more becoming
It is about staying tethered to the frequency you have already touched
It is about trusting what you cannot yet see
moving with the rhythm of a universe that always keeps its promises
and knowing that your presence itself is the prayer

Here you learn to stay
To remain unshaken in your alignment
to walk with a faith that is not fragile
to embody the timeless truth:
you are already whole, already home, already divine

The Bloom

There was no thunderclap of arrival
no ribbon stretched across a finish line
no crowd to declare you victorious

Only the quiet blooming
a thousand unseen moments
reshaping you from the inside out

The shift came in the quietest way
like dawn breaking without announcement
like petals opening without applause

You began to see differently
not through the eyes that measured and compared
but through the gaze of the soul

Here striving dissolves
the endless reaching loosens its grip
and something gentler rises to hold you

The soul has no need to prove
no need to be chosen
it has always been whole
it has always been enough

This is the vantage you enter now
where silence becomes companion not threat
where stillness carries more power than struggle
where every breath reminds you
you are already home

Rooted in Self While Loving

Even in the softest love
especially in the deepest love—
stay rooted in your own soil

Let your devotion never cost you, your direction
Let your tenderness never come at the price of your truth

As you open, stay anchored
Love deeply, but never drift from your own centre

Self Check-Ins

Pause often
Breathe inward
Ask:
Am I still anchored in my truth?
Is this desire arising from fullness—or from fear?
Let honesty be your compass
Even when it's unfamiliar

Solo Rituals

Keep sacred time for your own soul
Moments untouched by another's presence
Just you—
journaling beneath morning light
walking barefoot on earth
breathing in your own becoming
Rituals that remind you
who you are
outside of who you're loving

Visualization: The Temple of My Truth

Close your eyes and return to your own heart
Beneath your ribs, imagine a sanctuary—
softly lit, sacred, untouchable

This is your inner temple
No one enters unless invited
No one rearranges what lives here

See yourself tending to it with tenderness:
adorning it with truths, dreams, and quiet knowing
Let it hold your wholeness like a flame behind glass

Whenever you feel lost in love,
come back here
Breathe
Remember
Reclaim yourself gently

You were never meant to vanish
You were always meant to remain

Trusting What You Cannot Yet See

When you no longer betray yourself
something within begins to steady
a deep alignment that asks for no witness

You honour your truth even when it feels inconvenient
even when it costs you approval
even when solitude is your only companion

And slowly life bends to meet you
not through luck
not through chance
but through coherence

The universe does not mirror your wishing
it mirrors your being

When you are rooted in alignment
the right doors open without force
the right people arrive without chase
the old heaviness loosens and fades

Alignment is not about perfection
it is about trust
moving with the unseen rhythm
resting in a deeper order that cannot yet be measured

Here synchronicities become your language
soul nudges become your compass
clarity greets you in the quiet
and what once felt chaotic arranges itself into meaning

The Art of Stillness and Release

Letting go is not defeat
It is the soul's way of making space for what is yet to arrive
The unclenching of the hand
The pause before the bloom
The quiet opening that allows grace to enter

When you release the need to control—
to prove, to push, to demand—
you stop scattering your energy into a thousand directions
You begin to rest into the stillness that needs no performance
No striving can carry you where surrender already has

This stillness is the stance of the soul
Unmoved by comparison
Unshaken by delay
Unimpressed by urgency
It is here to remind you
the oak does not strain to become the oak
It grows because it cannot do otherwise

The ego clings because it fears emptiness
The soul releases because it knows fullness is its nature
To let go is not to lose
It is to align

Trust that life moves in a rhythm wiser than your plans
Stand in stillness and remember—
You are already held by what you cannot yet see

The Timeless Rhythm

Life moves in a rhythm older than time
The tides rise and fall without asking your permission
The moon waxes and wanes without your approval
The seasons turn whether you are ready or not

There is a current beneath all things
an eternal pulse that carries you

Whether you call it the universe
the simulation
life itself
or simply the mirror of your inner world—
it responds to you

To live in surrender is to trust a higher choreography
To allow endings to hold the seeds of beginnings
To let yourself be moved rather than forcing the dance

Life is not against you
It's happening for you
It has only been asking you to release the fight
to hear the music beneath the noise
and to join the rhythm that was always leading you home

The Surrendered Self

Surrender is no longer a practice
It becomes your nature

You do not release once and return to clinging
You soften again and again until softness becomes strength
until trust becomes your foundation

This is devotion to the unseen
A choosing of the current over the cage
A remembering that the river already knows its way to the sea

At this depth, surrender is not only letting go of people or plans
It is loosening your grip on identity itself
The small self that strives, compares, fears, and proves

Here, the soul takes the lead
and you rest in the rhythm that has always carried you
Each detour reveals its hidden perfection
Each delay hums with quiet orchestration
Each ending becomes a doorway instead of a grave

The surrendered self is free
because she does not need to control the unfolding
Her part is to stay aligned in essence
to keep her frequency clear
to meet each moment as it arrives
and to let life rise to meet her in return

The Courage to Step Beyond

Let go
Trust the flow
Believe it will all make sense

It sounds simple on paper
But simplicity does not mean easy

To release what you've clung to
To loosen the grip on what is known—
even if it has hurt you
even if it has kept you small—
requires a bravery most never touch

Because the unknown asks more of you
than the familiar ever will
It strips away the safety of certainty
It asks you to walk blindfolded
led only by faith

Most would rather suffer in what they know
than risk stepping into mystery
But not you
You have heard the whisper
You know there is more

So keep walking into the unknown
And never forget—
You are the avatar
the player
and the architect

In Hindsight, There Was Grace

What you clung to, became your weight
What you released became your wings

You've surrendered before—
even when you didn't know you were doing it
Remember the detour you didn't ask for
the door that slammed shut
the love that slipped away no matter how tightly you held on

At the time it felt like loss
like collapse
like something precious being stolen
But later—quietly, with time—
something gentler came
a deeper truth
a kinder love
a more honest version of you

Surrender rarely feels sacred in the moment
It feels like ashes on your tongue
But in hindsight
you see it
You see how the delay was protection
how the ending was mercy
how the collapse was a clearing
for something greater to take root

So when your hands tremble to release again
when your ego fights to hold on
let this remembering anchor you
Grace has always been threading your life together

Sacred Inquiry: In Hindsight, There Was Grace

Recall a time you longed deeply for something that never came

- How did it feel to stand in that ache?
- Looking back now, what arrived in its place?
  —Can you see how life was protecting or redirecting you?
- Write a letter to your past self from the vantage of today
  —What would you tell her in her moment of loss?

And now

- what in your present life feels uncertain, delayed, or unfinished?
- How might you hold it differently if you trusted grace is already at work?

Let your answers come slowly
without forcing
without judgment
This reflection is not about fixing the past
but about weaving it into the wholeness of your becoming

Creation in Alignment

You are a natural-born creator
It is not a skill you acquire—it is the true nature of your soul
Every thought, every breath, every choice writes itself into form
This truth has always lived in your bones

When you create from alignment, you are not forcing life to bend to your will
You are opening to the current already flowing through you
Manifesting is not a trick of the mind
It is the remembrance that your very being is generative
That to live awake is to live as a channel for beauty, love, and expansion

To create is to let the spark in your soul move into the world
It is to witness the unseen become seen
the inner frequency take shape in outer form
Not through striving, but through resonance
Not through demand, but through certainty

Let gratitude be the soil where your visions take root
Patience—the vibration that keeps them steady
Trust—the sun that draws them toward fullness

Creation in alignment is not about accumulation
It is about expression
It is about walking in harmony with the beat of life
and remembering that everything you truly need
was already humming within you

The Becoming Before the Receiving

Manifesting is not about getting what you want
It is about becoming the one who already holds it
Every desire is a spark of the soul
Every asking a call to remember who you truly are

The universe does not deliver your dreams out of timing
It waits—not to punish, but to tend to you
To prepare you, to shape you
Each pause, each delay, each detour
is a sacred midwife of your becoming

Even what feels like rejection
or redirection
is part of the choreography
Each test, each trial
pulls away what you are not
so that what you are may rise

You are never behind
You are never lost
You are always being positioned
always being prepared
to meet the life, you are calling forth

Alignment is the magnet—
the quiet embodiment of who you are
When your energy, your thoughts, your presence
resonate with your desire
the universe has no choice but to match you

Lessons That Echo

If a pattern reappears in different clothing
if a lesson keeps returning—
know this
It is not punishment
It is sacred persistence

The Universe will echo the same truth
until you live it in your bones

Sometimes it comes back
not because you failed before
but because you are now strong enough
soft enough, wise enough
to meet it anew

Everything in life is a spiral
Each turn brings you deeper into your essence
So do not resent the repetition
Receive it as invitation

Because the moment you truly choose yourself—
wholly, without hesitation
You are free

Free to rise beyond old stories
Free to love without grasping
Free to step into the timeline
that has always been waiting for your yes

Follow the Spark

You are at your truest self when you rest in the frequency of ease
Let go of the need to know how it all unfolds
Focus only on the next step before you—nothing more
In truth, there is no future—There is only now

The path is not hidden
It appears the moment you stop demanding to see the whole road
And remember—
you can never be lost
because you are the path itself

So pause and ask yourself:
What excites me most at this moment?

Don't overthink it
Don't measure its worth by how productive it seems
Simply follow it
with your whole being

If it's a walk in the park
a quiet nap
a dance in your kitchen
or curling up with a book—
let yourself say yes

Desire is not distraction—it is direction
It is how your soul whispers, *this way*

The spark may seem small
but when you follow it, life responds
Opportunities appear

Ideas unfold
Synchronicities gather at your feet

This is alignment
This is receptivity
This is creation in its purest form

Grateful for the Unseen

When you stop sulking over what isn't and begin bowing to what is
When your breath becomes a thank you
When your mornings open in reverence
and your heart hums with quiet awe—
you begin to touch the frequency of ease

Ease to receive
Ease to trust
Ease to believe that what you desire
was always yours by birthright

At this point, gratitude is no longer something you perform
It becomes the natural rhythm of your being

And from that place, gratitude for what you cannot yet see
flows as effortlessly as gratitude for what already lives in your hands

For the dreams still forming
The doors quietly waiting to open
The paths laying themselves beneath your feet—
you can already say thank you

Close your eyes
Breathe in possibility
Feel the richness of what is coming
without knowing the shape, without needing the when
Offer your heart a quiet thank you—
for the becoming
for the alignment
for the gifts already arriving
in the vibration of your trust

Sacred Reflection: The Pause Between Desires

Sometimes it feels hard to thank life for what has not yet appeared
Not because it isn't meant for you
but because some part of you does not believe it is already yours
Sit gently with this part of you—no fixing, just listening

When I try to feel gratitude for something not yet here:

- What part of me resists?
- Where in my body do I feel the discomfort—chest, belly, throat?
- What story does this part believe?
  That it's too soon? Too unrealistic? Too much?
- Whose voice is this—mine, or someone else's?

Breathe with it
Soften it with love, not shame

Now, step into the version of you who already lives this life
She is not performing gratitude—she is breathing it

Let your nervous system settle here
Let this become your home base

Because the simple truth is
The life you desire—
If it's not yours, whose is it?

Engrave this into your being—
Gratitude is not a performance of worthiness
It is the remembrance that you were always worthy to receive

Sacred Homecoming

What you once searched for outside
was here all along—
quiet, steady, waiting to be remembered

Every release, every surrender
was never a loss
but a return
a step closer to the centre of yourself

This is the homecoming—
to honour the versions of you who carried the weight,
to steady your heart when the noise grows loud,
to anchor in the self who has always known the way

She Walked Me Here

The past versions of you was never wrong
She simply did not yet know better
and still, she loved with all she had

There comes a moment when you stop trying to fix yourself
You stop digging through rubble for the exact crack
and instead you sit with your scars
trace them with tenderness
and whisper
I understand

Not every choice made in ache was a mistake
Not every soft yes was weakness
Even heartbreak was holy in its own way
Your past self wasn't broken
She was becoming

Because here is the truth
You would not be who you are now
rooted, radiant, resourced
without the version of you who stumbled and kept going
who once chased love but learned to become it
who gave too much but finally discovered her worth
who tried to be chosen but now chooses herself again and again

The goal was never to erase her
but to integrate her
to let her rest in your heart as a sacred chapter
not a shameful one
Because you cannot hate the girl you were
and love the woman you're becoming

So let the shame dissolve
let the regret breathe
and let compassion rise higher than pain ever could
She walked you here
She deserves to be honoured—not buried

Close your eyes
See her before you
tender, unarmoured, hopeful
Step forward and embrace her

Let her dissolve into your heart
not as a ghost but as a guide
not as someone left behind
but as light you now carry forward

Because every version of you
was worthy of love
And now, at last
you are wise enough to know that you are both the giver and the receiver
of that sacred love

When the Noise Gets Loud

No matter how far you've come, life will still test you
The path will not always be clear
There will be days when the fog thickens
when the voices around you grow louder than the voice within

In these moments, you may forget
You may feel unmoored, unsure, unsteady
This does not mean you have falling back
It means you are being invited to return

You are never without guidance
You carry a compass within you—your higher self
She is the steady flame that does not flicker, even when the winds rise

Visualization: Anchoring to the Higher Self

Find a quiet place where you will not be disturbed
Close your eyes and let your breath deepen
Imagine a soft golden light surrounding you
expanding from your heart until it fills the room

Before you, see her—your higher self
She looks like you, but steadier
Her eyes hold the wisdom of every lesson you have yet to live
Her presence radiates peace

Step closer until you stand face to face
Ask her what you need to remember in this moment
Listen—her guidance may come as words, as a feeling, as an image

Now imagine taking her hands in yours
Feel her steadiness transfer into you
Let her breath become your breath
her calm becomes your calm
her certainty becomes your anchor

Stay here until your body softens
until your heart feels rooted in trust
Know this: she is not separate from you
She is the you that has always been whole
the observer behind the awareness

When you are ready, open your eyes
Carry her presence with you
as the stillness that is stronger than striving
as the knowing that steadies you in the fog

The Living Prayer

To live as a living prayer is to embody everything you've reclaimed—
grace, strength, softness, depth, mystery, wholeness

It is no longer about being anything other than
simply you

Your frequency is the offering
Your presence is the legacy

Not built in grand gestures or achievements
but in the smallest choices—
the words you whisper to yourself when no one is listening
the tenderness you offer when old wounds rise
the courage to choose love over fear, again and again

You no longer need to seek sacred ground
You are the sacred ground
Every breath, every step, every intention is already an altar

You don't need to be loud to be unforgettable
You don't need the world to witness your becoming
Your devotion is enough

Let your legacy be how deeply you lived
Let it be how remarkably unique your path was
Let it be how safe others felt to return home to themselves—
because you dared to come home to you

A Ritual – The Living Prayer

This ritual is your vow to the highest version of you—
to your soul,
to your truth

You will need:
—a candle
—a mirror
—a journal

Set the space
Light the candle
Sit before the mirror with your journal nearby
Let the flame remind you of the spark within—
always burning, always there for you

Meet your eyes
Gaze softly into your reflection
Not to fix, not to judge
But to truly see—
to witness the woman who has risen,
the woman who has returned

Speak your vow aloud:
"I vow to live as the highest version of myself
I vow to honour the life I've been given
I vow to no longer dim, chase, or shrink
My presence is enough
My being is sacred
I am the living prayer"

A Final Reflection

One day, your footsteps will quiet
The rooms you once filled will fall silent
And your story will live only in the breath of others

Between this moment and that one
you are the sculptor of what remains
Each choice, each kindness, each truth spoken
is a brushstroke on the canvas of your legacy

Ask yourself:
—What kind of life do I want to leave behind?
—What energy do I want to be remembered for?
—How would I live if my very existence were my offering?

Journal Your Legacy

Take your journal and write freely about the energy, values, and impact you wish to leave behind—
not only for others, but for yourself

Imagine your future self ten years from now:
—What does she thank you for?
—What sacred choices did you make today for her?

This is not the end
This is your becoming
Your softest, fiercest, most honest self—
walking the earth as light,
as depth,
as a woman who remembers...

She is the prayer

A Final Whisper

This Is Your One Wild Life

Pause
Breathe in the miracle of now
This is not a rehearsal—
This is your one life

You cannot rewrite the beginning
But you can begin here
With grace in your spine
And devotion in your breath

Remember:
You owe no one a watered-down version of yourself
But you do owe yourself a life that feels true, full, and free

If this moment were the only thing guaranteed—
How would you live it?
What would you no longer delay?
What part of you would you finally stop hiding?

You are not here to repeat the same day for eighty years and call it a life
You are here to feel it all
To live it all
To let your days become the most honest love letter to your soul

You were made for this version of you
And this version of you was made for this moment

So go—
Choose beauty

Choose authenticity
Choose wholeness

Become the woman your past self prayed for
Become the one your future self thanks you for

There is only one of you in the entire universe
Let your life reflect that miracle

A Letter From My Heart to Yours

If you've arrived at these final pages, know this:
I am so deeply proud of you—
Not because you reached a final signpost,
but because you dared to walk through yourself

You felt
You faced
You softened
You released what was never yours
and remembered what always was

This kind of bravery is quiet
It rarely earns applause
Yet it births miracles

This journey was always about returning—
to the woman who lived beneath the ache and the doubt,
to the power you were born with but forgot to claim,
to the truth that was never lost,
only hidden beneath the weight of survival

I didn't write these words to teach you
I wrote them to remind you—
of your softness and your strength,
of your divine nature

You are not behind
You are not broken
You are right on time for your own becoming

So walk on, sacred woman
Romanticize the ordinary

Begin again as many times as you need
Let your life be slow
full of soul and drenched in truth

You are the prayer
You are the light
You are the quiet revolution

And the world is better because you remembered

With my whole heart,
Anjali

Printed in Dunstable, United Kingdom

71830077R00117